PRACTICE
CULTURAL CURRICULUM

Name: _____   Class: _____

Table of Contents

Introduction	2
Maya's Cultural Odyssey: A Tapestry of Appreciation and Unity	3
Unexpected Bonds: The Unveiling Connection of Sunil and Crystal	10
Viral Bonds: The Uncharted Territory of Crystal and Sunil's Friendship	18
The Ripple Effect: Unveiling the Science Behind the Joy of Kindness	25
Breaking Barriers: Jackie Robinson's Courageous Journey in Baseball	33
The Impact of Our Food Choices on Earth's Climate	41
Inspiring Murals: Nipsey's Everlasting Legacy	50
Claudette Colvin: Unheralded Pioneer of Civil Rights	59
Empowering Young Minds: Alexis Lewis and the Inventive Spirit	68
Evolving Social Preferences: Jenna's Experience with Online Networks	78
Survival Strategies: The Marvels of the Mariana Abyss	86
The Martian Expedition: Ciara and Roy's Dynamic Collaboration	94
Sonia's Encounter with Nature's Enchantment	103
The Impact of Compassion: Roger's Transformative Encounter	111
Whispers in the Texan Twilight	120
Rosa Parks: A Quiet Courage That Changed Society	129
Saturday Morning	140
A Complex History	151
The Musical Journey	162
Zooming Through Corvette History	172
NYS ELA Short Response Scoring Rubric	181

Introduction

Seventh graders, want to crush your ELA state exam? This workbook is for you! We've found the most important concepts from past exams and made them easy to understand. Plus, you'll learn how to become a better reader and writer. Let's show that test who's boss!

Guiding Notes:

- Target Vocabulary - these words appear in the readings and should be introduced as you're reading.

- Comprehension questions - these questions follow every passage to test your mastery.

- Writing prompt - after each text you'll have an opportunity to reflect on what you read. We recommend spending 15 minutes answering the prompt.

Maya's Cultural Odyssey: A Tapestry of Appreciation and Unity

Objective(s):
- Identify the main idea using supporting details from the short story, "*Maya's Cultural Odyssey: A Tapestry of Appreciation and Unity*".
- Construct a written response using evidence from the text describing how Maya's participation in a cultural festival at her school made her appreciate her culture as well as others.

ELA Standard(s):
- 7R2: Determine a theme or central idea of a text and analyze its development over the course of the text; summarize a text.
- 7R3: In literary texts, analyze how elements of plot are related, affect one another, and contribute to meaning. (RL)

Essential Question:
- How does Maya's participation in a cultural festival allow her to appreciate her culture as well as other cultures?

Target Vocabulary:
- Vibrant
- Swayed
- Fumbled
- Saw Duang
- Sarong
- Elegant
- Mesmerized
- Reluctantly

In the bustling hallways of her school, Maya found herself at the center of a vibrant cultural festival, an experience that would shape her appreciation for her own heritage and the rich tapestry of diverse cultures around her. This narrative unfolds the story of Maya's journey as she participated in this cultural extravaganza, answering the essential question of how her involvement allowed her to appreciate not only her own culture but also the myriad of others.

As the rhythmic beats of traditional music swayed through the air, Maya fumbled with the intricacies of putting on a sarong, a garment representing her cultural roots. Despite the initial hesitation, Maya soon found herself draped in the elegant fabric, embodying the essence of her heritage.

One of the highlights of the festival was the mesmerizing performance of the Saw Duang, a traditional Thai musical instrument. Maya, initially reluctant to participate, was drawn into the enchanting melodies, realizing the beauty and significance of her own cultural heritage.

Reluctance transformed into admiration as Maya witnessed the performances of other cultures. The diverse array of dances, languages, and traditions on display created a harmonious blend that transcended borders. Maya's appreciation expanded beyond her own roots, embracing the richness of the world's cultural diversity.

In the end, Maya emerged from the cultural festival with a newfound appreciation for her heritage and an enriched understanding of the world's cultural mosaic. The tapestry of colors and cultures woven together in that vibrant event left an indelible mark on Maya's perspective, fostering unity and appreciation for the diversity that makes each culture unique and valuable.

Comprehension Questions:

1. What is the setting of the story "Maya's Cultural Odyssey: A Tapestry of Appreciation and Unity"?

a) Maya's home
b) Maya's school
c) A cultural festival
d) An art museum

2. What is the significance of the sarong in the story?

a) It is a traditional Thai musical instrument
b) It represents Maya's cultural roots
c) It is an elegant fabric worn by all students
d) It is a tool used in vibrant dance performances

3. What is the role of Mr. Lem in the story "Ron and Sheila's Culinary Adventure: A Harmony of Perspectives in the First Sip"?

a) He is Ron and Sheila's neighbor
b) He is a spacecraft engineer
c) He is a grizzled chef guiding the culinary adventure
d) He is a mollusk enthusiast

Writing prompt:

Using two details as evidence from the text describing what does the term "culinary spacecraft" symbolize, and how does it contribute to the overall theme of the narrative?

PRACTICE
CULTURAL CURRICULUM

Unexpected Bonds: The Unveiling Connection of Sunil and Crystal

Objective(s):
- Analyze how elements of the plot allow for further understanding of meaning in "*Not Alone [The Weird Ones, #2]*" by Rick Coleman
- Construct a written response using evidence from the text describing how Sunil and Crystal's relationship allows Crystal to feel less alone because of her special talent.

ELA Standard(s):
- 7R3: In literary texts, analyze how elements of plot are related, affect one another, and contribute to meaning. (RL)

Essential Question:
- How does Sunil and Crystal's new found commonality allow for their friendship to grow throughout the story?

Target Vocabulary:
- Massive
- Grimaced
- Coincidence Insist
- Tremble
- Muttered
- Relieved

In the heart of the bustling seventh-grade hallways, a tale of unexpected friendship unfolds between Sunil and Crystal. This narrative delves into how their newfound commonality, arising from Crystal's special talent, becomes the foundation for a deep and meaningful connection, addressing the essential question of how this common ground allows their friendship to blossom.

Sunil, a seemingly ordinary teenager, discovered the extraordinary in Crystal. Her unique talent, a mysterious ability that set her apart, drew Sunil's attention. As Crystal demonstrated her skill, an uncanny coincidence revealed Sunil's hidden interest in the same domain. This shared fascination became the seed for their friendship to sprout and grow.

The massive impact of their common ground became evident as Crystal grimaced less, finding solace in Sunil's presence. The once-isolated feelings that accompanied her special talent transformed into a source of connection, shared with someone who understood the intricacies of her experience.

Through shared moments of coincidence and mutual understanding, Sunil and Crystal's friendship evolved. Sunil, refusing to let Crystal feel alone, insisted on being a pillar of support. Their bond deepened as Crystal's trembles of uncertainty were replaced by shared laughter and camaraderie.

In whispered conversations and moments of shared relief, Sunil and Crystal's friendship thrived. Crystal muttered her thoughts and fears to a friend who genuinely cared, transforming the once-isolated journey into a shared adventure.

As the story unfolds, the power of shared interests and mutual understanding becomes the cornerstone of Sunil and Crystal's friendship, illustrating how unexpected connections can bridge the gap between isolation and camaraderie.

Comprehension Questions:

1. What sets Crystal apart from others in the story "Unexpected Bonds: The Unveiling Connection of Sunil and Crystal"?

a) Her athletic abilities
b) Her mysterious special talent
c) Her academic achievements
d) Her musical prowess.

2. How does Sunil react to discovering Crystal's special talent?

a) He becomes jealous
b) He insists on keeping his distance
c) He grimaces in disapproval
d) He is drawn to her unique ability

3. How does Crystal's special talent initially make her feel?

a) Isolated and alone
b) Excited and proud
c) Indifferent and uninterested
d) Competitive and superior

Writing prompt:

How does the evolving friendship between Sunil and Crystal contribute to the overall message or lesson? Use two pieces of evidence from the text to support your response.

Viral Bonds: The Uncharted Territory of Crystal and Sunil's Friendship

Objective(s):
- Analyze how elements of the plot allow for further understanding of meaning in "*Viral Bonds: The Uncharted Territory of Crystal and Sunil's Friendship*" by Rick Coleman.
- Construct a written response using evidence from the text that describes the effects of "going viral" for Crystal and Sunil

ELA Standard(s):
- 7R3: In literary texts, analyze how elements of plot are related, affect one another, and contribute to meaning. (RL)
- 7R2: Determine a theme or central idea of a text and analyze its development over the course of the text; summarize a text. (RI & RL)

Essential Question:
- Crystal and Sunil's friendship grows because of their similarities; what are some of the effects on the friends of "going viral"?

Target Vocabulary:
- Unconcerned
- Doctored
- Grainy
- Levitating
- Pragmatic
- Claim
- Proactive
- Artificial Intelligence
- Bioengineering
- Striding
- Urgent
- Anxiously

In the realm of cyberspace, Sunil and Crystal's friendship takes an unexpected turn when their shared experiences become the talk of the virtual town. This narrative explores the effects of "going viral" on their lives and delves into the challenges and triumphs that arise from the newfound attention, answering the essential question of how the dynamics of their friendship are influenced by this digital phenomenon.

It all begins innocently enough - a video clip, grainy yet captivating, capturing a moment when Crystal's unique talent has her levitating, and Sunil, seemingly unconcerned, stands beside her. As this snippet finds its way onto various platforms, the duo becomes an internet sensation, their friendship the subject of speculation and admiration.

With each share and comment, the effects of this digital wildfire become evident. Crystal, once pragmatic and unconcerned about the virtual world, finds herself anxiously navigating the attention. Sunil, usually proactive and doctored in his approach to life, learns to stride confidently in the spotlight cast upon them.

The sudden claim to fame triggers an urgent need for both friends to define the boundaries of their shared exposure. Doctored stories and manipulated narratives emerge, challenging the authenticity of their friendship. In the midst of this chaos, the friends find themselves grappling with the impact of artificial intelligence in shaping public perception.

As the viral wave rolls on, Crystal and Sunil must confront bioengineering their friendship in the public eye. The challenges of maintaining authenticity in an artificially intelligent world become apparent, forcing the friends to be proactive in preserving the core of their bond.

Amidst the digital frenzy, "Viral Bonds" explores how the unconventional circumstances of going viral test the resilience of friendship and challenge the duo to navigate the uncharted territory of virtual fame.

Comprehension Questions:

1. What initially sets off the viral fame for Sunil and Crystal in "Viral Bonds: The Uncharted Territory of Crystal and Sunil's Friendship"?

a) Crystal's solo performance
b) A grainy video capturing Crystal's levitation
c) Sunil's proactive approach to social media
d) A doctored image showcasing their friendship

2. How does Crystal react to the sudden attention and fame in the virtual world?

a) Anxiously and concerned
b) Proactively and confidently
c) Unconcerned and indifferent
d) With urgency and skepticism

3. Referencing the story, what does the quote "Sunil, usually a pragmatic soul, finds himself swept up in the digital whirlwind of attention, striding confidently through the virtual spotlight" reveal about Sunil's character development?

a) Sunil becomes indifferent to the virtual attention
b) Sunil embraces the digital whirlwind with anxiety
c) Sunil maintains his pragmatic approach in the spotlight
d) Sunil becomes reserved and avoids the virtual world

Writing prompt:

How does the digital journey impact Sunil and Crystal's friendship, and what lessons can be drawn from their experience in the virtual world?

Use evidence from the text to support your response.

_____

_____

_____

_____

_____

_____

_____

_____

_____

PRACTICE
CULTURAL CURRICULUM

21

The Ripple Effect: Unveiling the Science Behind the Joy of Kindness

Objective(s):
- Analyze how scientists have found a variety of ways that being kind to others actually makes you feel good in the text, "*The Ripple Effect: Unveiling the Science Behind the Joy of Kindness*".
- Construct a written response using evidence from the text that supports the central idea of the text; kindness can amplify your feelings of happiness which will then make you more kind.

ELA Standard(s):
- 7R3: In informational texts, analyze how individuals, events, and ideas are introduced, relate to each other, and are developed. (RI)

Essential Question:
- What have researchers discovered about how acts of kindness improves a person's mood?

Target Vocabulary:
- Cunning
- Striatum
- Psychology
- Neuroscience
- Motivation
- Reciprocity

Once upon a time, in the realm of psychology and neuroscience, researchers delved into the intricate workings of the human brain. Among them was a protagonist, a curious soul keen on unraveling the mysteries of human behavior.

In the labyrinth of studies and experiments, our character stumbled upon a treasure trove of knowledge, discovering that acts of kindness had a magical ability to amplify feelings of happiness. This revelation led to a cascade of positive emotions, creating a beautiful cycle where happiness and kindness danced hand in hand.

The cunning researchers, armed with brain scans and behavioral experiments, ventured into the intricate pathways of the striatum—a region of the brain associated with pleasure and reward. What they found was astonishing. When individuals engaged in acts of kindness, the striatum lit up like a constellation of joy, releasing a symphony of neurotransmitters that fueled feelings of delight.

Motivated by this newfound understanding, our character explored the concept of reciprocity. The more kindness one bestowed upon the world, the more the world reciprocated with happiness. It was a dance of positive energy, a delightful exchange that echoed through the corridors of human connection.

The research unveiled the profound impact of kindness on mood improvement. Our character, now armed with this knowledge, embarked on a mission to spread kindness like seeds in the wind. The world transformed, one act of kindness at a time.

And so, the tale of the science behind the joy of kindness spread far and wide, leaving an indelible mark on the hearts and minds of those who embraced the simple yet powerful truth: kindness begets happiness, and happiness begets kindness.

In the end, our character realized that the true magic lay not just in the discovery but in the application—how kindness, like a potion, had the power to create a world where joy and compassion thrived, painting the canvas of humanity with the vibrant hues of reciprocity.

Comprehension Questions:

1. What is the central idea of the story "The Ripple Effect: Unveiling the Science Behind the Joy of Kindness"?

a) Kindness has no impact on happiness
b) Acts of kindness can amplify feelings of happiness
c) Happiness diminishes the desire to be kind
d) Reciprocity has no connection to human behavior

2. Which region of the brain is associated with pleasure and reward, as mentioned in the story?

a) Cerebellum
b) Amygdala
c) Hippocampus
d) Striatum

3. According to the story, what is the relationship between kindness and reciprocity?

a) Kindness hinders reciprocity
b) Reciprocity leads to less kindness
c) There is no connection between kindness and reciprocity
d) Kindness fosters a positive cycle of reciprocity

Writing prompt:

How can understanding the neuroscience and psychology behind acts of kindness influence individual behavior and contribute to building a more compassionate society?

Use evidence from the text to support your response.

_____
_____
_____
_____
_____
_____
_____
_____
_____
_____

Breaking Barriers: Jackie Robinson's Courageous Journey in Baseball

Objective(s):
- Analyze how the former baseball player, Jackie Robinson influenced the Major Leagues in, "*Breaking Barriers: Jackie Robinson's Courageous Journey in Baseball*".
- Construct a written response using evidence from the text that supports the central idea of the text; in spite of discrimination against Jackie Robinson, he fought against adversity as the first African American to play in the Major Leagues.

ELA Standard(s):
- 7R3: In informational texts, analyze how individuals, events, and ideas are introduced, relate to each other, and are developed. (RI)

Essential Question:
- What were some of the various ways that Jackie Robinson battled against racial discrimination throughout his life?

Target Vocabulary:
- Mound
- Diverse
- Poverty
- Integrated
- Minority
- Marred
- Acquitted
- Indication
- Prejudice
- Plagued
- Recruiting
- Barrier

- Admittance
- Adverse
- Inspired
- Civil Rights Movement

Once upon a diamond-shaped realm, the echoes of a bat meeting a ball resonated, weaving a tale of courage and resilience. In this narrative, our protagonist, Jackie Robinson, stood as a symbol of fortitude in the face of racial discrimination.

From the mound to the dugout, Jackie faced the adversities of being the first African American to play in the Major Leagues. His journey was marred by prejudice and the societal norms of his time. The baseball field, once a symbol of unity, was plagued by the divisive barriers of racism.

Jackie's arrival in the Major Leagues marked a momentous shift towards diversity and integration. The mere indication of his presence shattered the unwritten rules that had kept the sport divided. The recruiting of Jackie Robinson was not just about a talented athlete taking the field but a pivotal moment in the fight against discrimination.

Outside the confines of the baseball stadium, Jackie's life reflected the struggle against poverty and the harsh realities faced by minority communities. He became an inspiring figure not only for his prowess on the field but for his unwavering commitment to justice.

Jackie's battles against racial discrimination were not confined to the diamond. His acquittal and determination became an inspiration for the burgeoning Civil Rights Movement. He fought against adversity, breaking through the barrier that had denied admittance to countless talents based on the color of their skin.

As we delve into the pages of history, Jackie Robinson's legacy shines as a beacon of hope, a testament to the power of courage in the face of adversity. His integrated journey paved the way for future generations, leaving an indelible mark on the sport and society alike.

Comprehension Questions:

1. What is the central idea of the story "Breaking Barriers: Jackie Robinson's Courageous Journey in Baseball"?

a) The history of baseball in the Major Leagues
b) Jackie Robinson's prowess as a baseball player
c) The integration of African Americans in baseball
d) The challenges faced by minority communities in the Civil Rights Movement

2. What societal norms did Jackie Robinson challenge by joining the Major Leagues?

a) Economic disparities
b) Gender discrimination
c) Racial segregation
d) Educational inequalities

3. How did Jackie Robinson's acquittal impact the Civil Rights Movement?

a) It had no impact on the movement
b) It inspired and contributed to the movement
c) It led to increased discrimination
d) It resulted in a decline in civil rights activism

Writing prompt:

In what ways did Jackie Robinson's journey in baseball extend beyond the sport and contribute to broader societal changes, particularly in the fight against racial discrimination?

Use evidence from the text to support your response.

The Impact of Our Food Choices on Earth's Climate

Objective(s):
- Analyze how the food choices we make affects the Earth in *"The Impact of Our Food Choices on Earth's Climate"*.
- Construct a written response using evidence from the text that supports the central idea of the text; how the food that is produced and consumed can have environmental costs.

ELA Standard(s):
- 7R3: In informational texts, analyze how individuals, events, and ideas are introduced, relate to each other, and are developed. (RI)

Essential Question:
- According to the article, what do scientists claim about the environmental costs of producing food?

Target Vocabulary:
- Resources
- Irrigate
- Crop
- Fertilizer
- Pollution
- Manure
- Greenhouse gasses
- Fermentation
- Ruminant
- Potent
- Emissions
- Equivalent
- Vegetarians
- Vegan
- Consumption

- Mitigation
- Sustainability
- Groundwater
- Erosion
- Graze

Once upon a time in a small town, there lived a curious seventh-grader named Alex. One day in science class, the teacher introduced an intriguing article titled "Your Food Choices Affect Earth's Climate," and Alex couldn't wait to dive into the fascinating world of environmental science.

The article discussed the essential question: According to scientists, what do they claim about the environmental costs of producing food? As Alex delved into the text, the answer became clear.

In the story, the protagonist, Alex, learned about the intricate web of connections between the food we consume and the environmental toll it takes. The narrative began with a detailed exploration of the various resources involved in food production, such as water, land, and energy. Alex discovered that large-scale crop cultivation often requires extensive irrigation, leading to the depletion of groundwater resources.

The article emphasized the role of fertilizers in crop production, explaining how their use contributes to pollution in water bodies. Alex learned that the runoff from fertilized fields can contaminate rivers and lakes, impacting aquatic ecosystems. The term "erosion" caught Alex's attention, describing how the overuse of land for agriculture leads to soil erosion, degrading the quality of arable land.

The story further unfolded the environmental costs associated with livestock farming. Alex encountered the term "ruminant" and discovered that certain animals, like cows, produce potent greenhouse gases during digestion. The article elaborated on how methane emissions from these animals contribute significantly to climate change. The connection between manure and methane emissions was highlighted, portraying the impact of livestock on Earth's atmosphere.

As Alex continued reading, the narrative explored the concept of fermentation in agriculture, emphasizing its role in greenhouse gas emissions. The article discussed mitigation strategies, introducing terms like "vegetarians" and "vegans" as individuals who choose diets with lower environmental impacts. Alex learned that reducing meat consumption could be a sustainable solution to address the environmental costs of food production.

The protagonist discovered the importance of considering the carbon footprint of different foods. The article introduced the concept of emissions equivalent, providing a measure to compare the environmental impact of various food choices. Alex was fascinated by the idea of making informed decisions to promote sustainability.

In the end, Alex realized that understanding the environmental costs of food production is crucial for making responsible choices. The story concluded with a call to action, encouraging readers to be mindful of their consumption habits to contribute to a more sustainable and environmentally friendly future.

Comprehension Questions:

1. What contributes to the pollution of water bodies in the story?

a. Greenhouse gasses
b. Irrigation
c. Erosion
d. Fermentation

2. Which term refers to animals that produce potent greenhouse gasses during digestion?

a. Vegetarians
b. Ruminants
c. Vegans
d. Mitigation

3. What is suggested as a sustainable solution to address the environmental costs of food production in the story?

a. Increased meat consumption
b. Heavy use of fertilizers
c. Vegan and vegetarian diets
d. Ignoring carbon footprints

Writing prompt:

Explain the relationship between food choices and environmental impact as highlighted in the story. Provide examples from the text to support your response.

_____

_____

_____

_____

_____

_____

_____

_____

_____

_____

Inspiring Murals: Nipsey's Everlasting Legacy

Objective(s):
- Analyze how street art as murals created by Nipsey Hussle can bring a community together in "Inspiring Murals: Nipsey's Everlasting Legacy".
- Construct a written response using evidence from the text that supports the central idea of the text; how a person's legacy can live on through artwork (murals) and continue to inspire others.

ELA Standard(s):
- 7R3: In informational texts, analyze how individuals, events, and ideas are introduced, relate to each other, and are developed. (RI)

Essential Question:
- According to the informational text, how did the legacy of Nipsey Hussle unify people as seen through murals and artwork?

Target Vocabulary:
- Activist
- Inspiring
- Legacy
- Entrepreneur
- Motivation
- Interactions
- Dispute
- Sought-after
- Philanthropic work
- Ethos
- Effusive
- Emissions
- Uniting
- Homage

- Spearheaded
- Initiative
- Unveil
- Memorial
- Advocate
- Solidifying
- Grieve

In the vibrant streets of Los Angeles, a seventh-grade student named Maya delved into a captivating article titled "Nipsey's Everlasting Legacy," eager to uncover the profound impact of art on people's lives.

The story began by exploring the essential question: How did the legacy of Nipsey Hussle unify people as seen through murals and artwork? As Maya read on, the answer unfolded through the evidence presented in the text.

The protagonist discovered that Nipsey Hussle, a renowned activist, entrepreneur, and advocate for change, left behind a powerful legacy that extended far beyond his philanthropic work. Nipsey's ethos of inspiring others and fostering positive change was a central theme in the article, highlighting how his life and actions served as a motivational force for many.

Maya found out that Nipsey was not only an entrepreneur but also a sought-after figure in the community, known for his philanthropic initiatives. The text described his interactions with the community, emphasizing how he sought to unite people through his endeavors, solidifying his position as an inspiring figure.

The article shed light on Nipsey's efforts to bring positive change to his neighborhood, spearheading initiatives that aimed to reduce emissions of violence and create a sense of unity. Maya learned that the murals honoring Nipsey were not merely artistic expressions but a form of homage to his advocacy and impact.

As Maya continued reading, the narrative unfolded the aftermath of Nipsey Hussle's tragic demise and the disputes that arose in his community. However, the story highlighted how the murals became a source of comfort and inspiration for those grieving, transforming into a memorial that celebrated Nipsey's life and contributions.

The text showcased how the murals served as a lasting testament to Nipsey's legacy, inspiring others to continue his work and advocate for positive change. Maya discovered that the artwork became a focal point for the community, symbolizing the unity and motivation derived from Nipsey's life.

In the end, Maya understood that the legacy of Nipsey Hussle lived on through the captivating murals that adorned the streets of Los Angeles. These artistic expressions not only served as a visual tribute but also as a powerful force that continued to inspire and unite people in the pursuit of positive change.

Comprehension Questions:

1. What role did Nipsey Hussle play in the community, as highlighted in the story?

a. Professional athlete
b. Philanthropic entrepreneur and activist
c. Famous actor
d. Environmental scientist

2. How did the murals honoring Nipsey Hussle impact the community after his tragic demise?

a. They led to more disputes and disagreements.
b. They became a source of comfort and inspiration.
c. They were ignored by the community.
d. They were criticized for their lack of artistic value.

3. What did Nipsey Hussle's legacy aim to achieve, according to the text?

a. Increase emissions of violence
b. Create division within the community
c. Unite people and advocate for positive change
d. Disregard artistic expressions

Writing prompt:

Explain the significance of the murals in solidifying Nipsey Hussle's legacy and inspiring the community, providing examples from the text to support your response.

_____

_____

_____

_____

_____

_____

_____

_____

_____

_____

PRACTICE
CULTURAL CURRICULUM

Claudette Colvin: Unheralded Pioneer of Civil Rights

Objective(s):
- Analyze how Claudette Calvin affected the Civil Rights Movement in "*Claudette Colvin: Unheralded Pioneer of Civil Rights*".
- Construct a written response using evidence from the text that supports the central idea of the text; Claudette Calvin's activism went unnoticed in comparison to other Civil Rights leaders and how she inspired others.

ELA Standard(s):
- 7R3: In informational texts, analyze how individuals, events, and ideas are introduced, relate to each other, and are developed. (RI)

Essential Question:
- According to the informational text, how did Claudette Colvin's actions inspire others, and how did Civil Rights leaders respond?

Target Vocabulary:
- Boycott
- Fined
- Voluntarily
- Segregated
- Abolitionist
- Activist
- Injustices
- Jim Crow
- Oppression
- Integration
- Enterprises
- Black Power
- NAACP
- Shunned

- Gravitas
- Inherently
- Impressive
- Pragmatism
- Fore

In the pages of history, the lesser-known but formidable figure Claudette Colvin emerged as the protagonist of a compelling narrative. As a seventh-grade student named Marcus delved into the story titled "Claudette Colvin: Unheralded Pioneer of Civil Rights," he discovered the profound impact of her activism and the challenges she faced.

The central idea of the text revolved around Claudette Colvin's activism, which often went unnoticed compared to other prominent Civil Rights leaders. The essential question guiding Marcus through the text was: How did Claudette Colvin's actions inspire others, and how did Civil Rights leaders respond?

As Marcus read on, he encountered evidence supporting the notion that Claudette's bravery and resistance to segregation inspired others in the fight against racial injustices. The narrative began with a vivid depiction of Claudette's voluntary act of defiance on a Montgomery bus, refusing to give up her seat to a white passenger.

The story highlighted Claudette's activism as an abolitionist, bravely challenging the oppressive Jim Crow laws that enforced racial segregation. Despite being fined for her actions, Claudette's resolute stand against injustice went unnoticed by many, overshadowed by the later, more publicized actions of Rosa Parks.

Marcus discovered that Claudette's courage and refusal to accept segregation on buses set the stage for the Montgomery Bus Boycott, a pivotal event in the Civil Rights Movement. The text explored how Claudette's actions inspired others, leading to a collective effort to boycott segregated public transportation.

As Marcus continued reading, he learned that Civil Rights leaders, including those associated with the NAACP, acknowledged the significance of Claudette's contributions. However, due to pragmatic considerations and concerns about public perception, they chose to rally behind Rosa Parks as the face of the boycott.

The text delved into the complexities of the era, where the Black Power movement gained momentum, and leaders made strategic decisions to navigate the challenges posed by an inherently discriminatory system. Despite Claudette's achievements being shunned by some, her legacy endured as a symbol of resistance and activism.

The story concluded with Marcus gaining a newfound appreciation for Claudette Colvin's impressive role in the Civil Rights Movement. He understood that while some leaders took the fore, Claudette's early actions laid the groundwork for a more integrated and just society, leaving an indelible mark on the fight against racial oppression.

Comprehension Questions:

1. What was Claudette Colvin fined for in the story?

a. Voluntarily refusing to give up her seat on a bus
b. Promoting segregation on public transportation
c. Advocating for the Jim Crow laws
d. Joining the Black Power movement

2. How did Claudette Colvin's actions contribute to the Civil Rights Movement?

a. By promoting segregation
b. By boycotting public transportation
c. By accepting injustice
d. By supporting the Jim Crow laws

3. Why did some Civil Rights leaders choose to rally behind Rosa Parks instead of Claudette Colvin?

a. Claudette's actions were not considered significant.
b. Rosa Parks had more gravitas.
c. Claudette supported segregation.
d. Rosa Parks initiated the Jim Crow laws.

Writing prompt:

Using text evidence, explain the complexities faced by Civil Rights leaders in choosing to highlight Rosa Parks over Claudette Colvin. How did this decision impact the perception of the Civil Rights Movement during that era?

_____

_____

_____

_____

_____

_____

_____

_____

_____

Empowering Young Minds: Alexis Lewis and the Inventive Spirit

Objective(s):
- Analyze how Alexis Lewis thinks that more kids could help solve problems in the world in *"Empowering Young Minds: Alexis Lewis and the Inventive Spirit"*.
- Construct a written response using evidence from the text that supports the central idea of the text; more kids should be given the opportunity to invent and create as a way to solve the world's problems.

ELA Standard(s):
- 7R2: Determine a theme or central idea of a text and analyze its development over the course of the text; summarize a text. (RI & RL)

Essential Question:
- According to the informational text, why does Alexis Lewis think that kids make good inventors?

Target Vocabulary:
- Patent
- Travois
- Refugees
- Patent-pending
- Canister
- Advocate
- Curriculum
- Perspective
- Motivated
- Humanitarian
- Physics
- Obsessively
- Revolving

- Fascinating
- Voraciously
- Invaluable
- Fabricated
- Pneumatic
- Accuracy
- Abysmal
- Thomas Edison
- Alexander Graham Bell

In the realm of innovation, a seventh-grade student named Dylan embarked on a journey through the pages of a captivating article titled "Empowering Young Minds: Alexis Lewis and the Inventive Spirit." The narrative unveiled the remarkable story of Alexis Lewis and her fervent belief that more kids should be given the opportunity to invent and create as a means to address the world's problems.

The central idea of the text revolved around Alexis Lewis's perspective that young minds possess unique qualities that make them excellent inventors. Dylan was guided by the essential question: Why does Alexis Lewis think that kids make good inventors?

As Dylan delved into the story, he encountered compelling evidence supporting Alexis's viewpoint. The article began by introducing Alexis as a motivated teenager with a voracious appetite for knowledge, who approached problem-solving with a fresh and imaginative perspective. Her fascination with physics and an insatiable curiosity led her to explore solutions that others might overlook.

The protagonist discovered that Alexis was not merely an inventor but also an advocate for empowering young minds. She believed that incorporating inventing into the curriculum could cultivate the inventive spirit in students, offering a valuable and hands-on educational experience. Alexis saw young inventors as invaluable contributors to solving real-world problems, and her advocacy extended to challenging the abysmal accuracy of underestimating the potential of young minds.

As Dylan continued reading, the narrative unfolded Alexis's inventions, from a patent-pending canister to a pneumatic device designed to aid refugees. Her creations were not only fascinating but also fabricated with precision, demonstrating the accuracy and depth of thought that young inventors could bring to the table.

The text introduced terms like "Travois" and "Humanitarian" in the context of Alexis's inventions, showcasing her commitment to addressing global challenges. Dylan learned that Alexis's perspective on inventing was rooted in her humanitarian goals, reflecting the belief that the inventive spirit could be harnessed to make a positive impact on the world.

The story touched upon the historical context of inventors, mentioning iconic figures like Thomas Edison and Alexander Graham Bell, but Alexis's story stood out as a modern example of how young minds could contribute significantly to the field of invention.

In the end, Dylan understood that Alexis Lewis's belief in the inventive capacity of young minds was grounded in the notion that their fresh perspectives, motivated curiosity, and untapped creativity could offer innovative solutions to some of the world's most pressing problems. The article concluded with a call to action, advocating for a shift in perspective and an acknowledgment of the invaluable contributions young inventors can make to shape a brighter future.

Comprehension Questions:

1. What does Alexis Lewis advocate for in the story?

a. Suppressing young inventors' creativity
b. Ignoring the curriculum
c. Empowering young minds through inventing in the curriculum
d. Dismissing the potential of young inventors

2. What is mentioned as one of Alexis Lewis's inventions?

a. Revolving door
b. Pneumatic device for refugees
c. Alexander Graham Bell's telephone
d. Thomas Edison's light bulb

3. What quality does Alexis Lewis believe young inventors possess?

a. Inattention
b. Untapped creativity and fresh perspectives
c. Aversion to knowledge
d. Lack of curiosity

Writing prompt:

Explain how Alexis Lewis's perspective on empowering young inventors aligns with her humanitarian goals. Provide examples from the text to support your response.

_____

_____

_____

_____

_____

_____

_____

_____

_____

_____

Evolving Social Preferences: Jenna's Experience with Online Networks

Objective(s):
- Analyze how technology can affect our daily lives in the interview, "*Evolving Social Preferences: Jenna's Experience with Online Networks*".
- Construct a written response using evidence from the text that supports the central idea of the text; some users have deactivated their accounts because of their lackluster feelings towards Facebook.

ELA Standard(s):
- 7R2: Determine a theme or central idea of a text and analyze its development over the course of the text; summarize a text. (RI & RL)

Essential Question:
- According to the interview conducted by NPR, why is Facebook losing its allure for users despite members continuing use on the platform?

Target Vocabulary:
- Disenchantment
  Envious
- Passive Use
- Wallflower
- Social Butterfly
- Intrusive
- Faux Pas
- Norm

In the realm of virtual connections, a seventh-grade student named Liam delved into the pages of an intriguing article titled "Evolving Social Preferences: Jenna's Experience with Online Networks." The narrative unraveled the story of Jenna, shedding light on the disenchantment some users feel towards Facebook, leading to account deactivation.

The central idea of the text revolved around Jenna's experience and the evidence supporting the notion that some users have deactivated their accounts due to their lackluster feelings towards Facebook. Liam explored the essential question: According to the interview conducted by NPR, why is Facebook losing its allure for users despite members continuing use on the platform?

As Liam read through the text, he discovered that Jenna, like many others, experienced a sense of disenchantment with Facebook. The platform, once a vibrant virtual space for connections, had lost its appeal, prompting some users to take the drastic step of deactivating their accounts.

The narrative delved into the concept of passive use, where users became wallflowers on the platform rather than active participants. Jenna's experience echoed the sentiments of those who felt envious or left out when witnessing the highlight reels of others, contributing to a sense of disconnection.

The text highlighted Jenna's shift from being a social butterfly to a more reserved and introspective user. Facebook's intrusive nature, with constant notifications and updates, began to feel like a faux pas in the evolving norms of online social interactions. Liam discovered that Jenna's decision to deactivate her account was influenced by the changing landscape of social preferences and a desire for more authentic connections.

As Liam continued reading, the narrative touched upon the broader trend observed by NPR in their interviews, indicating that Jenna's experience was not an isolated case. Many users shared similar feelings of disenchantment, prompting them to reevaluate their engagement with Facebook despite its continued use by millions.

In the end, Liam gained a nuanced understanding of the evolving dynamics of online social networks. Jenna's story became a microcosm of the broader trend where users, despite the norm of continued use, were choosing to step back due to their changing preferences and the platform's perceived shortcomings. The article concluded with a reflection on the ever-shifting landscape of online connections and the impact it has on individual experiences.

Comprehension Questions:

1. What term is used in the story to describe users who are more reserved and less active on Facebook?

a. Social butterflies
b. Wallflowers
c. Envious users
d. Intrusive participants

2. According to the text, why did some users, including Jenna, deactivate their Facebook accounts?

a. Due to the platform's popularity
b. Because of their envious feelings towards others
c. In response to an increase in authentic connections
d. Despite a lackluster feeling towards Facebook

3. What term is used in the story to describe Facebook's constant notifications and updates that users find intrusive?

a. Faux pas
b. Disenchantment
c. Norm
d. Passive use

Writing prompt:

Explain the shift in Jenna's social media experience from being a social butterfly to a wallflower. How does this shift reflect broader trends in users' attitudes towards Facebook, as discussed in the text?

Use evidence from the text to support your response.

Survival Strategies: The Marvels of the Mariana Abyss

Objective(s):
- Analyze how scientists have discovered sea creatures in the deepest place on Earth, the Mariana Trench, in *"Survival Strategies: The Marvels of the Mariana Abyss"*.
- Construct a written response using evidence from the text that supports the central idea of the text; sea creatures have adapted to their environment in the Mariana Trench.

ELA Standard(s):
- 7R3: In informational texts, analyze how individuals, events, and ideas are introduced, relate to each other, and are developed. (RI)

Essential Question:
- How have the sea creatures in the Mariana Trench adapted for survival in such an inhospitable environment?

Target Vocabulary:
- Spare
- Abyss
- Vessels
- Peer
- Vast
- Inhospitable
- Expanses
- Swarming
- Translucent
- Colossal
- Gnashing
- Adapted
- Mashed

In the depths of oceanic exploration, a seventh-grade student named Mia delved into the fascinating world presented in an article titled "Survival Strategies: The Marvels of the Mariana Abyss." The narrative unveiled the remarkable adaptations of sea creatures in the Mariana Trench, showcasing their ability to thrive in an otherwise inhospitable environment.

The central idea of the text revolved around the evidence supporting the notion that sea creatures in the Mariana Trench have adapted to their environment for survival. Mia explored the essential question: How have the sea creatures in the Mariana Trench adapted for survival in such an inhospitable environment?

As Mia read through the text, she discovered the vast expanses of the Mariana Trench, an abyss in the ocean where colossal pressures and inhospitable conditions create a challenging environment for life. Despite these challenges, the narrative provided evidence of how sea creatures had not merely survived but thrived in this extreme underwater realm.

The text described the adaptations of swarming translucent organisms that peer through the dark abyss, showcasing their ability to navigate and locate prey in the absence of sunlight. Mia encountered details about colossal creatures that had spare vessels filled with fluids to counteract the intense pressure, allowing them to explore the depths without being crushed.

Mia learned about the gnashing jaws of deep-sea dwellers that had adapted to a diet of mashed-up organic matter falling from the surface. These unique adaptations reflected the incredible diversity of life in the Mariana Trench and the ingenious strategies sea creatures had developed for survival.

As Mia continued reading, the narrative highlighted the peer-reviewed scientific studies that unveiled the mysteries of this underwater realm. Scientists had observed and documented the various ways in which sea creatures had adapted to the inhospitable conditions, shedding light on the marvels of the Mariana Abyss.

In the end, Mia marveled at the resilience and adaptability of the sea creatures in the Mariana Trench. The article concluded with a sense of wonder, leaving Mia with a newfound appreciation for the incredible adaptations that enable life to flourish in the most challenging and mysterious corners of the ocean.

Comprehension Questions:

1. What is the Mariana Trench described as in the story?

a. Swarming abyss
b. Vast expanses of sunlight
c. Colossal vessels
d. Inhospitable environment

2. How do sea creatures in the Mariana Trench adapt to the lack of sunlight?

a. By having spare vessels filled with fluids
b. By swarming in large groups
c. By relying on vast expanses of sunlight
d. By avoiding the abyss

3. What is mentioned as a diet strategy for some deep-sea dwellers in the Mariana Trench?

a. Colossal vessels
b. Mashed-up organic matter
c. Translucent adaptations
d. Swarming behavior

Writing prompt:

Explain the significance of the adaptations described in the story for sea creatures in the Mariana Trench. How do these adaptations contribute to their survival in such an extreme environment?

The Martian Expedition: Ciara and Roy's Dynamic Collaboration

Objective(s):
- Analyze the theme of the story by examining the plot to allow for further understanding of meaning in "*Mission to Mars*" by Sheela RamanThe Martian Expedition: Ciara and Roy's Dynamic Collaboration".
- Construct a written response using evidence from the text that supports the claim that Ciara and Roy work well as a team

ELA Standard(s):
- 7R3: In literary texts, analyze how elements of plot are related, affect one another, and contribute to meaning. (RL)
- 7R2: Determine a theme or central idea of a text and analyze its development over the course of the text; summarize a text. (RI & RL)

Essential Question:
- How does the use of teamwork allow for a successful mission to Mars for Roy and Ciara?

Target Vocabulary:
- Spectators
- Frontier
- Salutations
- Embark
- Groundbreaking
- Voyage
- Colossal
- Generate
- Vastness
- Amid
- Finite
- Claustrophobic

\
- Donned
- Arid
- Manned
- Craters
- Generated
- Hurtling

In the realm of interplanetary exploration, a seventh-grade student named Liam embarked on the pages of an article titled "The Martian Expedition: Ciara and Roy's Dynamic Collaboration." The narrative unfolded the tale of a groundbreaking mission to Mars, highlighting the evidence that Ciara and Roy's effective teamwork played a pivotal role in its success.

The central idea of the text revolved around the evidence supporting the claim that Ciara and Roy worked well as a team during the mission to Mars. Liam sought answers to the essential question: How does the use of teamwork allow for a successful mission to Mars for Roy and Ciara?

As Liam read through the text, he discovered that the duo, Ciara and Roy, had donned their spacesuits with salutations to the spectators, signifying the beginning of their extraordinary voyage to the Martian frontier. The narrative generated a vivid image of the colossal spacecraft hurtling through the vastness of space, manned by the two intrepid explorers.

Amid the claustrophobic confines of the spacecraft, Ciara and Roy generated an atmosphere of collaboration and camaraderie. The finite space didn't hinder their ability to work seamlessly as a team. Liam encountered details about the barren and arid Martian landscape, marked by craters and challenges that required their collaborative efforts to navigate successfully.

The text highlighted moments of the mission where Ciara and Roy's teamwork shone through, whether it was in the meticulous generation of data or the effective coordination required to address unexpected challenges. Liam learned that their ability to work in unison, leveraging each other's strengths, was instrumental in overcoming obstacles and ensuring the success of their groundbreaking mission.

As Liam continued reading, the narrative emphasized the importance of teamwork in interplanetary exploration. Ciara and Roy's collaboration extended beyond the confines of their spacecraft, impacting their interactions with mission control and enhancing their problem-solving capabilities in the face of the Martian unknown.

In the end, Liam marveled at the synergy between Ciara and Roy that propelled the mission to Mars to new heights. The article concluded with a sense of accomplishment, leaving Liam with a deeper understanding of the crucial role teamwork plays in venturing into the uncharted frontiers of our solar system.

Comprehension Questions:

1. How did Ciara and Roy begin their mission to Mars, according to the story?

a. Amid barren landscapes
b. With salutations to spectators
c. In claustrophobic conditions
d. Without donning spacesuits

2. What challenges did Ciara and Roy face on the Martian frontier?

a. Abundant resources
b. Smooth and even terrain
c. Finite space in the spacecraft
d. Lack of teamwork

3. What is highlighted as an impact of Ciara and Roy's teamwork during the mission?

a. Hindered problem-solving capabilities
b. Limited interactions with mission control
c. Effective coordination and data generation
d. Groundbreaking challenges on Mars

Writing prompt:

Explain how Ciara and Roy's teamwork contributed to the success of the mission to Mars. Provide examples from the text to support your response.

Use evidence from the text to support your response.

_____

_____

_____

_____

_____

_____

_____

_____

_____

_____

Sonia's Encounter with Nature's Enchantment

Objective(s):
- Analyze the theme of change in the story by examining the plot to allow for further understanding of meaning in *"Sonia's Encounter with Nature's Enchantment"*.
- Construct a written response using evidence from the text that supports the author's purpose for including details about the allure of nature. Use two details from the story to support your response.

ELA Standard(s):
- 7R3: In literary texts, analyze how elements of plot are related, affect one another, and contribute to meaning. (RL)
- 7R2: Determine a theme or central idea of a text and analyze its development over the course of the text; summarize a text. (RI & RL)

Essential Question:
- How does the allure of nature allow Sonia to change her mindset?

Target Vocabulary:
- Forego
- Dreary/dreariness
- Insistence/insisted
- Accounting firm
- Suburbs
- Amid
- Chaos
- Constantly
- Thorough
- Ajar
- Inclined
- Untamed
- Thicket

In the bustling world of literary exploration, a seventh-grade student named Emma delved into the pages of an article titled "Sonia's Encounter with Nature's Enchantment." The narrative unfolded the tale of Sonia's quest to find Salinger, weaving in the allure of nature and how it played a pivotal role in transforming her mindset.

The central idea of the text revolved around the evidence supporting the author's purpose for including details about the allure of nature. Emma explored the essential question: How does the allure of nature allow Sonia to change her mindset?

As Emma read through the text, she discovered Sonia's dreary existence amid the chaos of suburban life, constantly immersed in the demands of her accounting firm job. The narrative painted a vivid picture of Sonia's life, where the insistence of routine and the unyielding suburban landscape fostered a sense of monotony and discontent.

One day, Sonia found herself inclined to forego her usual routine and ventured into an untamed thicket, seeking solace amid nature's embrace. The text described the allure of the thicket, with the air filled with the fragrance of wildflowers and the rustling of leaves offering a welcome respite from the constant demands of her structured life.

Sonia's encounter with the natural world prompted a change in her mindset. Amid the untamed beauty of the thicket, she felt a sense of tranquility and connection that had been missing from her life. The author insisted on the thorough transformation Sonia experienced as she allowed herself to be enveloped by the beauty of nature.

As Emma continued reading, she observed Sonia's internal shift as the allure of nature served as a catalyst for self-discovery. The narrative highlighted how Sonia's mindset evolved from the confines of her suburban routine to a more open and introspective outlook, free from the dreariness that had permeated her existence.

The thicket's untamed beauty, with its secrets hidden in every leaf and flower, served as a metaphor for Sonia's own journey towards self-discovery. The article concluded with a reflection on the transformative power of nature and how Sonia's encounter with the untamed landscape had a lasting impact on her mindset.

In the end, Emma marveled at the author's purposeful inclusion of details about the allure of nature in Sonia's story. The article left her with a deeper understanding of how nature, in its untamed beauty, can serve as a powerful force for change, offering solace and inspiration in the midst of life's chaos.

Comprehension Questions:

1. Why does Sonia venture into the untamed thicket, according to the story?

a. Due to the insistence of routine
b. To escape her suburban life
c. To find Salinger
d. Inclined to forego nature

2. What impact does Sonia's encounter with nature have on her mindset?

a. It reinforces the dreariness of her routine
b. It doesn't affect her mindset
c. It prompts a transformative shift
d. It increases her insistence on chaos

3. What is emphasized as the allure of the thicket in the story?

a. The constant demands of routine
b. The fragrance of wildflowers and rustling leaves
c. The chaos of suburban life
d. The dreariness of untamed beauty

Writing prompt:

Explain the significance of the untamed thicket in Sonia's transformation. How does the allure of nature contribute to her change in mindset? Provide examples from the text to support your response.

_____

_____

_____

_____

_____

_____

_____

_____

_____

The Impact of Compassion: Roger's Transformative Encounter

Objective(s):
- Analyze the theme of change in the story by examining the plot to allow for further understanding of meaning in "*The Impact of Compassion: Roger's Transformative Encounter*".
- Construct a written response using evidence from the text that determines the theme of change throughout the short story and how this theme is developed over the course of the text.

ELA Standard(s):
- 7R3: In literary texts, analyze how elements of plot are related, affect one another, and contribute to meaning. (RL)
- 7R2: Determine a theme or central idea of a text and analyze its development over the course of the text; summarize a text. (RI & RL)

Essential Question:
- How is Roger's character affected by Mrs. Luella Bates Washington Jones' compassion throughout the text?

Target Vocabulary:
- Blue-jeaned sitter
- Pocketbook
- Permit
- Great mind
- Frail
- Willow-wild
- Half-nelson
- Kitchenette-furnished room
- Roomers
- Suede
- Day-bed
- Presentable

- Gas plate
- Ice box
- Barren
- Stoop

In the urban landscape of unexpected connections, a seventh-grade student named Mia embarked on the pages of an article titled "The Impact of Compassion: Roger's Transformative Encounter." The narrative unfolded the tale of Roger and Mrs. Luella Bates Washington Jones, highlighting the theme of change and how it developed throughout the text.

The central idea of the text revolved around the evidence supporting the theme of change, specifically focusing on how Mrs. Jones's compassion affected Roger's character. Mia delved into the essential question: How is Roger's character affected by Mrs. Luella Bates Washington Jones' compassion throughout the text?

As Mia read through the text, she encountered Roger, the blue-jeaned sitter with a frail appearance, attempting to snatch Mrs. Jones's pocketbook. However, instead of retaliating, Mrs. Jones surprised Roger with her compassion. She did not permit him to escape but, in an unexpected twist, took him to her kitchenette-furnished room.

The narrative described Mrs. Jones's great mind at work, recognizing that Roger's actions stemmed from more profound needs. The rooms and barren atmosphere of Mrs. Jones's home provided a stark contrast to the suede, day-bed, gas plate, and icebox, highlighting the disparity between their lives.

Mia observed the development of the theme of change as Mrs. Jones's compassion began to influence Roger. Despite his initial intentions, he found himself in the willow-wild embrace of Mrs. Jones's kindness rather than facing the consequences of his actions. The half-nelson grip of punishment was replaced with an unexpected lesson in responsibility and gratitude.

As Mia continued reading, the narrative unfolded the transformation of Roger's character. Mrs. Jones, through her actions and words, presented Roger with the opportunity to change. The presentable appearance of the room mirrored the change taking place within Roger—a change facilitated by the unexpected compassion he experienced.

The article emphasized the impact of Mrs. Jones's compassion, not only on Roger's immediate actions but also on his perspective and understanding of empathy. The story concluded with Roger leaving Mrs. Jones's home with more than just the suede shoes he had attempted to steal—a newfound sense of responsibility and a changed outlook on life.

In the end, Mia marveled at the way the theme of change permeated the narrative, driven by Mrs. Jones's compassion. The article left her with a profound understanding of how acts of kindness can transform not only individual actions but also the very core of one's character.

Comprehension Questions:

1. What prompts Mrs. Luella Bates Washington Jones to take Roger to her home?

a. Roger's insistence
b. Compassion for his situation
c. A permit she needs to issue
d. An invitation for tea

2. What is the significance of the room in Mrs. Jones's home where she takes Roger?

a. It is barren and unwelcoming
b. It mirrors the half-nelson grip of punishment
c. It represents the great mind of Mrs. Jones
d. It symbolizes the change taking place within Roger

3. What does Roger leave Mrs. Jones's home with, besides the suede shoes he attempted to steal?

a. A permit
b. A presentable appearance
c. A gas plate
d. A newfound sense of responsibility

Writing prompt:

Explain the impact of Mrs. Luella Bates Washington Jones's compassion on Roger's character development. How does this encounter shape Roger's actions and perspective throughout the story?

Provide examples from the text to support your response.

Whispers in the Texan Twilight

Objective(s):
- Analyze the theme of change in the story by examining the plot to allow for further understanding of meaning in "*Whispers in the Texan Twilight*".
- Construct a written response using evidence from the text that shows how the author uses suspense throughout the text to contribute to the meaning of the story.

ELA Standard(s):
- 7R3: In literary texts, analyze how elements of plot are related, affect one another, and contribute to meaning. (RL)
- 7R2: Determine a theme or central idea of a text and analyze its development over the course of the text; summarize a text. (RI & RL)

Essential Question:
- How does Carlos' absence contribute to suspense in the story?

Target Vocabulary:
- Host
- Gardenias
- Addicted
- Curfew
- Suspiciously
- Fruitless
- Perplexed
- "Space cadet"
- Inherently
- Absent-minded
- Benefit of the doubt
- Urge
- Capacity

- Desolate
- Raptly
- Spate
- Bewildered
- Varied
- Intruders
- Diagnosable
- Residents
- Afflicted
- Discern

In the vast expanse of Texan twilight, a seventh-grade student named Sofia embarked on the captivating pages of an article titled "Whispers in the Texan Twilight." The narrative unfolded the mysterious tale of Carlos's absence, revealing how the author skillfully employed suspense to deepen the meaning of the story.

The central idea of the text revolved around the evidence supporting the author's use of suspense, particularly focusing on how Carlos's absence contributed to the enigma. Sofia explored the essential question: How does Carlos' absence contribute to suspense in the story?

As Sofia read through the text, she discovered the setting— a Texan town caught in the spell of a curious night. The residents, raptly engaged in their nighttime routines, became suspiciously aware of Carlos's inexplicable absence. The gardenias that usually adorned his porch now lay desolate, casting an air of bewilderment over the usually tight-knit community.

The author masterfully wove a spate of varied reactions among the residents, each afflicted with a sense of perplexity. Carlos, often deemed a "space cadet," had an inherent capacity to captivate attention, making his absence all the more noticeable. Sofia discerned how the author strategically created suspense by withholding information about Carlos's whereabouts, leaving the residents in a state of uncertainty.

The text described how the urge to uncover the truth lingered among the residents, who were inherently curious about Carlos's unexplained disappearance. Some offered the benefit of the doubt, suggesting that he might be absent-mindedly lost in the beauty of the Texan night. Others, however, harbored suspicions that hinted at the presence of intruders in the tranquil town.

As Sofia continued reading, she observed how the suspense deepened with each passing moment of Carlos's absence. The fruitless search for answers left the residents in a state of suspense, yearning to unravel the mystery that had enveloped their quiet Texan night.

The narrative explored the concept of curfew as the night deepened, further amplifying the suspense surrounding Carlos's disappearance. The author's deliberate choice to keep Carlos's whereabouts undisclosed heightened the tension, adding to the overall sense of mystery.

In the end, Sofia marveled at the author's ability to use suspense as a narrative tool, skillfully crafting an atmosphere of intrigue and anticipation. The article left her with a sense of eagerness, wondering about the resolution of the enigma that had unfolded in the Texan twilight.

Comprehension Questions:

1. What contributes to the suspense in the Texan twilight, according to the story?

a. Carlos's gardenias in full bloom
b. Residents' varied reactions to the night
c. The presence of intruders
d. The residents' inherent capacity for curiosity

2. How do the residents react to Carlos's absence, initially?

a. They offer the benefit of the doubt
b. They become inherently suspicious
c. They ignore the situation
d. They are perplexed by the gardenias

3. What element of the Texan night contributes to the suspense, according to the story?

a. A desolate garden
b. Residents raptly engaged in their routines
c. The author's capacity for suspense
d. Carlos's absence and the mysterious night

Writing prompt:

Explain the impact of Carlos's absence on the overall atmosphere of the Texan town. How does the author effectively use suspense to engage the reader and create a sense of mystery in the story?

Provide examples from the text to support your response.

_____

_____

_____

_____

_____

_____

_____

_____

_____

Rosa Parks: A Quiet Courage That Changed Society

Objective(s):
- Analyze how Rosa Parks's character and contributions are interconnected and changed society, *"Rosa Parks: A Quiet Courage that Changed Society"*.
- Construct a written response using evidence from the text describing the impact that Rosa Parks's decision to refuse to give up her seat led to a chain of events that transformed society.

ELA Standard(s):
- 7R3: In informational texts, analyze how individuals, events, and ideas are introduced, relate to each other, and are developed. (RI)

Essential Question:
- Who was Rosa Parks and what contributions did she make to society?

Target Vocabulary:
- Segregation
- Confines
- Imparted
- Activism
- Subsequent
- Steadfastness
- Constitutionality
- Plaintiffs
- Precedent
- Dismantling
- Pivotal
- Yearned

Rosa Parks: The Quiet Courage that Changed Society

Introduction

Rosa Parks, often referred to as the "Mother of the Civil Rights Movement," is a name etched into the annals of history for her pivotal role in challenging racial segregation in the United States. Her act of defiance on December 1, 1955, when she refused to give up her seat on a bus to a white man in Montgomery, Alabama, sparked a revolution that reverberated far beyond the confines of that bus. This article explores the life, legacy, and profound contributions of Rosa Parks to American society and the global struggle for civil rights.

Early Life and Influences

Rosa Louise McCauley Parks was born on February 4, 1913, in Tuskegee, Alabama. Growing up in the racially segregated South, she was exposed to the harsh realities of discrimination from a young age. Her grandparents, who had been enslaved, imparted to her a strong sense of dignity and self-respect. Her mother, a teacher, and her father, a carpenter and skilled tradesman, instilled in her the values of education and hard work.

Rosa Parks's early experiences with racism deeply affected her and played a significant role in shaping her later activism. She attended a segregated school and witnessed firsthand the injustices endured by the African American community in the Jim Crow South. These early experiences sowed the seeds of her commitment to the fight for equality and justice.

The Montgomery Bus Boycott

On the fateful evening of December 1, 1955, Rosa Parks, a seamstress on her way home from work, took a seat in the "colored" section of a Montgomery city bus. When a white man boarded the bus and the "whites only" section filled up, the driver ordered Rosa and three other African American passengers to vacate their seats. Rosa Parks refused, and her refusal ignited a firestorm that would change the course of history.

Parks's arrest and subsequent trial for violating Montgomery's segregation laws galvanized the African American community in Montgomery. The Montgomery Improvement Association, led by a young minister named Dr. Martin Luther King Jr., organized a citywide bus boycott in protest of Parks's arrest and the broader issue of racial segregation on public transportation. The boycott, which lasted for 381 days, demonstrated the collective power of nonviolent resistance.

Rosa Parks's steadfastness in the face of adversity became a symbol of courage and resilience. Her actions inspired countless others to join the struggle for civil rights. The Montgomery Bus
Boycott not only led to the desegregation of Montgomery's buses but also marked the beginning of a larger movement for racial equality in the United States.

The Legal Battle and the Supreme Court's Decision

While Rosa Parks is most famous for her role in the Montgomery Bus Boycott, her contributions to the civil rights movement extended beyond that historic event. She played a crucial role in challenging segregation laws through the legal system. Her arrest and subsequent court case became a significant test of the constitutionality of segregation.

In Montgomery, Parks was found guilty of violating segregation laws and fined $10. Her conviction was appealed, and the case eventually made its way to the United States Supreme Court. In December 1956, the Supreme Court ruled in favor of Parks and her fellow plaintiffs, declaring that segregation on public buses was unconstitutional.

The Supreme Court's decision in Browder v. Gayle marked a major legal victory against segregation and set a precedent for challenging racial discrimination in public facilities. Rosa Parks's willingness to stand up for her rights and pursue legal action was instrumental in breaking down the legal barriers that upheld segregation.

National Recognition and Continued Activism

Rosa Parks's courage and determination did not go unnoticed. She became a symbol of the civil rights movement and received widespread recognition for her contributions. In 1956, just a few months after the successful conclusion of the Montgomery Bus Boycott, Parks met with prominent civil rights leaders, including Dr. Martin Luther King Jr., and received the NAACP's Spingarn Medal for her courageous actions.

However, her activism also came at a personal cost. Rosa Parks and her family faced threats and harassment, forcing her to relocate to Detroit, Michigan, in 1957. Despite these challenges, she continued to work tirelessly for civil rights. In Detroit, she joined the staff of Congressman John Conyers, where she served as a secretary and receptionist for over two decades.

Parks also remained actively involved in various civil rights organizations, including the Southern Christian Leadership Conference (SCLC) and the NAACP. Throughout the 1960s and beyond, she participated in protests and demonstrations aimed at ending racial discrimination and promoting social justice.

Legacy and Impact

Rosa Parks's legacy is immeasurable. Her actions and contributions to the civil rights movement had a profound impact on American society and the world at large. Here are some key aspects of her enduring legacy:

Inspiration: Rosa Parks's bravery served as an inspiration to countless individuals who were inspired to stand up against injustice and discrimination. Her simple act of refusing to give up her seat empowered others to take a stand for their rights.

Catalyst for Change: The Montgomery Bus Boycott, triggered by Parks's arrest, marked the beginning of a new era in the civil rights movement. It demonstrated the power of nonviolent protest and paved the way for the broader struggle for civil rights.

Legal Precedent: Rosa Parks's case, Browder v. Gayle, set a legal precedent that contributed to the dismantling of segregation laws in the United States. Her willingness to challenge segregation through the courts played a pivotal role in achieving legislative change.

Symbol of Courage: Rosa Parks became a symbol of courage and resilience, not just in the United States but around the world. Her name is synonymous with the fight for civil rights and social justice.

Continued Activism: Even after the success of the Montgomery Bus Boycott, Rosa Parks remained committed to the cause of civil rights. Her involvement in various civil rights organizations and ongoing activism demonstrated her unwavering dedication to the struggle for equality.

Conclusion

Rosa Parks's contribution to society goes far beyond her single act of defiance on a Montgomery bus. Her courage, determination, and commitment to justice made her a beacon of hope for millions of people who yearned for a more equitable and inclusive society. Through her actions, Rosa Parks helped ignite a movement that would challenge and eventually dismantle the systemic racism and segregation that plagued the United States.

Today, Rosa Parks's legacy continues to inspire individuals and movements around the world. Her story serves as a reminder that one person, armed with courage and conviction, can spark transformative change and leave an indelible mark on history. Rosa Parks will forever be remembered as a symbol of quiet but unyielding courage, a woman whose refusal to give up her seat led to a more just and inclusive society for all.

Comprehension Questions:

1. Why is Rosa Parks often referred to as the "Mother of the Civil Rights Movement"?

    a. She had many children who became civil rights activists.
    b. Her actions catalyzed the Montgomery Bus Boycott and inspired the broader movement.
    c. She initiated the first-ever civil rights protest.
    d. She founded the Civil Rights Movement organization.

2. Why did Rosa Parks's case, Browder v. Gayle, make its way to the United States Supreme Court?

    a. She wanted to be a Supreme Court justice.
    b. She had influential connections in the legal system.
    c. Her case was highly publicized and attracted national attention.
    d. She wanted to challenge the local government's authority.

3. Which word below BEST describes Rosa Parks?

    a. Courageous
    b. Resilient
    c. Uninfluential
    d. Both a and b.

Writing prompt:

Using evidence from the text, describe the impact that Rosa Parks's decision to refuse to give up her seat led to a chain of events that transformed society. Describe what those other events/effects were.

Saturday Morning

Objective(s):
- Analyze the character transformation that Celia underwent throughout the story by examining the plot to allow for further understanding in "*Saturday Morning*".
- Construct a written response using evidence from the text describing how Celia was able to merge her Spanish school world and her school friends' world together, helping her appreciate her culture even more.

ELA Standard(s):
- 7R3: In literary texts, analyze how elements of plot are related, affect one another, and contribute to meaning. (RL)

Essential Question:
- How did Celia undergo a character transformation in the story? Who helped her do this?

Target Vocabulary:
- Commotion
- Relentless
- Animated
- Vociferous
- Intensive
- Decipher
- Absent-mindedly
- Retorted

The honking was relentless. The bustling city streets were absolutely packed with people, cyclists, and cars. Shop vendors were shouting loudly trying to get Celia's attention as she tried to push through the crowded sidewalk.

She was going to be so late for school.

"CELIA!" She heard her name through the commotion. "Celia! Aiden! Breakfast is ready! It's time to wake up. You need to eat before you go to Spanish school!"

Ah, she wasn't late... yet. Those sounds were the screeching of her alarm clock and her mother's wake-up call, so Celia jumped out of bed and flew downstairs.

In the kitchen, her mom and grandparents were in the midst of an animated discussion about their plans for the luncheon they were hosting for their friends the next day. Celia quickly greeted everyone and accepted a breakfast burrito from her grandfather. Then she grabbed her backpack and rushed to the door, running her fingers through her slightly wavy brown hair.

"Thanks, Abuelito! ¡Hasta luego!" Celia said, waving to her grandfather before she dashed out. "I'll be back!"

Celia hoisted her backpack over her shoulder as she walked to the bus stop. Since she was little, Celia had spent every Saturday morning at Spanish school. Today, as she sat on the bus for the short ride, she recalled her vociferous complaints when she was younger about what a pain it was to have to wake up before 8 AM on Saturdays. Growing up, it had felt so unfair that she had to devote so much of her weekend learning about the Spanish language and culture while her "weekday school" friends could sleep late, then play sports or video games all day. It had always made her feel a little bit different. She had friends at Spanish school too, but the two worlds never really seemed to mix, and she sometimes felt like she lived two lives.

Now that she was in middle school, however, Celia had to admit that she had grown to love her Saturdays at Spanish school. Her family spent each summer in Spain, and she always had an awesome time in Madrid, partly because she could really speak the language, thanks to all those Saturdays. All that she'd learned over the years in Spanish
school had really helped her connect with her Spanish family and friends. Plus, this past year she had taken flamenco dance intensively, and she loved teaching the younger kids on Saturdays now that she'd become a teaching assistant. Every now and then she spotted a young student who reminded her of herself when she was younger, and it made her feel a sense of pride in how she chose to spend her weekends.

Celia's first tasks at school were to assist with the morning language class for the kindergarteners, then take them to the gym for salsa dancing, where they would learn the basics of the dance. After that, everyone headed back to the classroom for a music lesson. Celia pulled out her guitar to sing along with the teacher, leading the little kids in a round of Spanish nursery songs. All that activity was followed by lunch, after which Celia returned to the gym to teach a dance workshop for the older elementary-aged kids.

It was a long day, because Spanish Saturday school didn't end till 3 PM. When dismissal time finally rolled around, Celia breathed a sigh of relief, then hopped on the bus to Olivia's house, where her friends were working on their group project for science class.

Celia pulled off her headphones as she approached the front door.

"Hi, gang," she cheerfully greeted her three classmates gathered in the living room.

"Hey, Celia!" said a lanky boy with short, dark hair, who slapped her playfully on the back.

"Yo, Aiden!" Celia responded, then picked up a thick folder that her friend Liam tossed at her from across the coffee table.

"We're so glad you're here," Olivia said, "because we're a little stuck on how to wire this part to the motor. Can you take a look?"

Aiden turned on some music while Celia and Olivia tried to decipher the robotics instruction book and took turns assembling the parts and soldering the wires. Liam was busy taking photos to document their efforts for their eventual presentation.

Finally, the friends took a break to eat some of the pizza that Olivia's mom had brought in. Celia placed the robot-in-progress on the floor and absent-mindedly sang along to the music as she fiddled with the remote control.

"Hey, what is this song about?" Liam asked.

Celia looked up, puzzled, and asked, "What do you mean?"

"It's in Spanish, isn't it?" Liam asked. "Which means, Celia, that you're the only one here who understands the words."

Celia hadn't noticed that her study pals were listening to a Spanish pop playlist—she hadn't even fully registered that she'd been singing along. "Wow, guys, I didn't know you liked Spanish music!"

The others laughed. "Are you kidding? These beats are amazing!" said

Aiden, as he pretended to sing along—but of course, he didn't have a clue as to what the lyrics were about.

"You want to know what the singers are saying?" Celia asked, still a little stunned that her "weekday school" friends were so into Spanish pop.

All three friends immediately exclaimed, "Yeah!"

Pleasantly surprised, she replied, "Okay, in this one, the singer is talking about the beauty of life and appreciating every moment."

"Aww!" Olivia said, "I had no idea. I just liked the song."

"It's got such a catchy tune," said Liam. "Ba-baam-baam-ba!"

For the next 30 minutes, Olivia, Liam, and Aiden kept asking about the meaning of the lyrics of several other songs, and Celia did her best to translate the Spanish lyrics in the songs they heard.

"It's so cool that you can understand this stuff," Aiden sighed, "and translate it so well."
"And get this," Olivia exclaimed, "Celia also knows some of the dance steps!"

"No way!" Liam cried out, "so, can you dance like the Spanish artists? Listen, isn't this a good time for a dance break? Now you can show us some Spanish dance moves!"

"As a matter of fact," Celia replied as she jokingly twirled around, "I was practicing exactly that at Spanish school this morning."

The classmates headed for the backyard where they could stretch and spread out. As they giggled, Celia led them through some Spanish dance routines, and soon they were moving along.

"You're a pretty good teacher, Celia," Liam remarked.

"And you guys are pretty good students—almost as good as the little ones I taught today!" Celia retorted. "Soon you'll be ready to dance like pros!"

Olivia's mom poked her head into the backyard, and when she saw everyone dancing, she said, admiringly, "Wow! You look just like a Spanish pop group in one of those music videos!"

"Yeah!" Olivia said, "we should call ourselves The Innovators!"

"Thanks for teaching us the moves and what the songs are saying," Aiden chimed in. "If our science project wins, maybe we can celebrate with a Spanish food and music party!"

"Yes, let's do it!" Liam crowed. "Can you help us arrange something fun, Celia? I'll make the playlist!"

"Sure!" Celia replied, smiling to herself. For a long time, what she learned in Saturday school had only seemed useful around her Spanish family and friends… but now, it was feeling more like something to share and enjoy with her classmates, too. She laughed, and added, "You bring the tunes, and I'll bring the moves!"

Comprehension Questions:

1. How did Celia feel about her experiences in Spanish school on Saturday mornings in the beginning of the story?

    a. She feels that her friends from her weekday school and Spanish school are all connected.
    b. She feels like she leads two different lives because her weekday friends and Spanish school friends never really mix.
    c. She feels a bit disconnected from her Spanish school.
    d. She doesn't want to mix any of her friends together.

2. What role does music and dance play in the story?
    a. They are hobbies that Celia pursues for fun.
    b. They serve as a way to bridge cultural differences and connect with friends.
    c. They are only mentioned briefly and have no significant impact on the plot.
    d. They are used as tools for academic learning in the Saturday school.

3. Read the following sentence from the text. What can be concluded from the text? Choose the best answer.

    "For a long time, what she learned in Saturday school had only seemed useful around her Spanish family and friends… but now, it was feeling more like something to share and enjoy with her classmates, too."

    a. Celia is excited to finally learn that her two worlds can connect, and she can share her Spanish culture because her classmates showed that they value cultures that are different from their own.
    b. Celia is unhappy that she has to share her Spanish culture with her classmates.
    c. Celia is nervous that her classmates won't accept her for who she is.
    d. Celia thinks that her classmates will make fun of her and won't appreciate what she is sharing

Writing prompt:

Using evidence from the text, describe how Celia was able to connect her Spanish school world and her school friends' world together.

A Complex History

Objective(s):
- Analyze the historical context and how it relates to the themes of land, assimilation, and activism for Native Americans in the text, *"A Complex History: Native Americans and U.S. Policy in the Late 1800s to Early 1900s"*.
- Construct a written response using evidence from the text describing the challenges and resilience of Native American communities during the late 1800s and early 1900s.

ELA Standard(s):
- 7R3: In informational texts, analyze how individuals, events, and ideas are introduced, relate to each other, and are developed. (RI)

Essential Question:
- How were Native Americans marginalized? How did their resilience help them overcome their challenges?

Target Vocabulary:
- Juncture (a particular point in time)
- Indigenous (native to a land from the earliest time)
- Burgeoning (beginning to grow rapidly)
- Inadequate (lacking quality/insufficient)
- Communal (shared by all members of a community)
- Assimilate (become part of the rest of society or another culture)
- Surplus (amount of something left over/excess)
- Encroachment (intrusion on a person's rights or territory)
- Disenfranchising (deprive someone of the right to vote or have another privilege)
- Disparities (differences in treatment, especially ones that are unfair)
- Revitalize (to bring life and vitality back to something)

PRACTICE
CULTURAL CURRICULUM

The relationship between Native Americans and the United States during the late 1800s and early 1900s is a story of both resilience and struggle. This period marked a critical juncture in the history of indigenous peoples on the North American continent as they grappled with the far-reaching impact of U.S. policies. While the previous text touched on key events and policies, this narrative delves deeper into the multifaceted aspects of this historical era.

Changing Lives and Lands

The late 1800s saw significant shifts in Native American lifestyles and land ownership. With westward expansion and the burgeoning growth of the United States, Native American communities found themselves increasingly marginalized. The dispossession of their ancestral lands became a pressing concern, and the U.S. government employed various tactics to achieve this end.

One such tactic was the reservation system, which confined Native American tribes to designated areas, often far from their original territories. While some tribes managed to negotiate treaties that allowed them to retain some degree of autonomy on these reservations, many found themselves subjected to harsh conditions and insufficient resources. These reservations became a microcosm of the challenges Native Americans faced during this period, including economic hardship, limited access to education, and inadequate healthcare.

Economic Transformation and the Dawes Act

The late 19th century brought significant economic changes to the United States, which had ripple effects on Native American communities. The Dawes Act of 1887, also known as the General Allotment Act, was a reflection of this economic transformation. It aimed to break up tribal communal land ownership and promote individual land ownership and agriculture among Native Americans.

Under the Dawes Act, Native American lands were divided into smaller parcels and distributed to individual tribal members, with the hope that they would adopt European-style farming practices. While this policy sought to assimilate Native Americans into mainstream American society, it had complex consequences. Many Native Americans were not familiar with Western style agriculture and faced difficulties in adapting to this new way of life.

Furthermore, the allocation of "surplus" land to non-Native settlers resulted in further loss of tribal territories. By 1932, Native Americans had lost a substantial portion of their land, which had been in their possession for generations.

Assimilation through Education

Education played a pivotal role in the U.S. government's efforts to assimilate Native American children into American society. Indian boarding schools, often established on or near reservations, were central to this strategy. These schools aimed to erase Native American culture and replace it with European-American norms.

Students at these boarding schools were required to adopt Western clothing, cut their hair, and abandon their native languages and traditions. This assimilationist approach had profound consequences for Native American identity and cultural preservation. Many students endured emotional trauma and cultural dislocation as they were torn between their indigenous heritage and the demands of assimilation.

Resilience and Cultural Preservation

While U.S. policies sought to undermine Native American cultures, indigenous communities displayed remarkable resilience in preserving their traditions. Despite the challenges they faced, many tribes continued to pass down their languages, stories, and ceremonies from one generation to the next. Native American elders played a critical role in this preservation, ensuring that the cultural flame continued to burn.

Additionally, resistance movements emerged to protect tribal sovereignty and resist further encroachment on indigenous lands. Prominent figures like Sitting Bull, Crazy Horse, and Geronimo led their communities in efforts to defend their way of life against the encroachment of U.S. settlers and the U.S. Army.

The Power of Alliances and Activism

As the 19th century gave way to the 20th, Native American communities began to form alliances and engage in activism to address the pressing issues they faced. The Society of American Indians, founded in 1911, was one of the earliest pan-Indian organizations, advocating for Native American rights and social justice.

Simultaneously, Native Americans contributed to the United States' efforts during World War I. Their service in the military allowed many to gain new perspectives on citizenship and their place in American society, even as they continued to advocate for their own rights.

The 1924 Indian Citizenship Act: A Complex Victory

In 1924, the U.S. Congress passed the Indian Citizenship Act, also known as the Snyder Act, which granted citizenship to all Native Americans born in the United States. This was a significant milestone in recognizing the rights of indigenous peoples, but it came with complexities.

Some Native Americans welcomed citizenship as a means to gain voting rights and a stronger political voice. However, others were wary, fearing that this recognition was a double-edged sword. They worried that it might further assimilate them into a society that had long sought to erase their distinct cultural identities.

Moreover, the granting of citizenship did not automatically eliminate the challenges Native Americans faced at the state level. Many states continued to impose restrictions on Native American voting rights, disenfranchising them until the 1965 Voting Rights Act provided federal protection for their right to vote.

The Meriam Report and the Indian Reorganization Act

In 1928, the Meriam Report exposed the harsh conditions faced by Native Americans and highlighted the detrimental effects of government policies. The report paved the way for the Indian Reorganization Act of 1934, also known as the Wheeler-Howard Act. This legislation sought to rectify some of the injustices inflicted on Native American communities.

The Indian Reorganization Act allowed tribes to reestablish self-governance and regain control over their land. It encouraged the preservation of cultural traditions and provided resources for economic development and infrastructure improvement on reservations. This marked a turning point in U.S. policy, recognizing the importance of tribal self-determination and cultural heritage.

Continuing Challenges and Progress

Today, Native American communities continue to face significant challenges. Economic disparities, healthcare disparities, and issues related to land and resource management persist. However, there have been notable achievements as well. Some Native American entrepreneurs and businesses have thrived, contributing to the economic development of their communities.

Efforts to revitalize and preserve Native languages and cultures have gained momentum, with tribal schools and cultural centers playing a crucial role in this resurgence. Furthermore, legal victories in the realm of tribal sovereignty and land rights have reinforced the rights of indigenous nations.

In recent decades, there has been a growing recognition of the need to respect indigenous knowledge and practices, particularly in environmental conservation and land management. Collaboration between Native American tribes and federal and state governments has begun to reflect a more inclusive and equitable approach.

Conclusion

The history of Native Americans and U.S. policy during the late 1800s to early 1900s is a complex and multifaceted one, marked by both oppression and resilience. Native American communities faced numerous challenges as they navigated the shifting sands of U.S. expansionism and assimilation efforts.

However, their rich cultural heritage, their determination to preserve their identity, and their ability to forge alliances and advocate for their rights have enabled them to overcome many obstacles. While contemporary challenges persist, there is a growing awareness of the need to honor tribal sovereignty, support cultural revitalization, and foster collaboration between Native American nations and the broader American society.

In recognizing the complexities of this history, we can move toward a future that respects and upholds the rights and contributions of Native Americans, acknowledging that their heritage is an integral part of the tapestry of American history.

Comprehension Questions:

1. What is one example of how Native American communities have worked to preserve their cultural heritage despite the challenges they faced?

    a. By completely abandoning their traditional practices and languages.
    b. By selling their ancestral lands to non-Native settlers.
    c. By forming alliances with European-American settlers.
    d. By passing down their languages, stories, and ceremonies to younger generations.

2. Based on the information provided in the text, what can be inferred about the impact of the Indian Reorganization Act of 1934 on Native American communities?

    a. It led to the complete eradication of tribal self-governance.
    b. It resulted in the forced relocation of Native American tribes.
    c. It allowed tribes to regain control over their land and promoted cultural preservation.
    d. It significantly expanded the boarding school system.

3. Which theme below was not deeply explored in the text about Native Americans and their complex history?

    a. Music and dance
    b. Land
    c. Citizenship and activism
    d. Assimilation

Writing prompt:

Citing evidence from the text, describe both the challenges and resilience of Native American communities during the late 1800s and early 1900s.

The Musical Journey

Objective(s):
- Identify the problem and solution from the story, *"The Musical Journey"*.
- Construct a written response using evidence from the text to describe at least one of the themes that was highlighted in the story.
-

ELA Standard(s):
- 7R2: Determine a theme or central idea of a text and analyze its development over the course of the text; summarize a text. (RL)

Essential Question:
- How does Jesse and his musical journey transform in the story?

Target Vocabulary:
- Conductor
- Diligently
- Uninspired
- Signaling
- Resonates
- Sympathetically
- Disheartened
- Expressive
- Reignited
- Improvisation
- Liberated

Every Friday afternoon, the halls of Willowbrook Middle School were filled with the sound of music. Today was no exception as 40 middle schoolers gathered in the music room, led by their conductor, Mrs. Anderson. They were diligently practicing an arrangement of "Mars" from Gustav Holst's "The Planets."

Among the students, there was one named Jesse Reynolds who sat in the middle of the first trumpet section. While his peers seemed to be lost in the music, soaring among the stars, Jesse felt grounded and uninspired.

Suddenly, a sharp screech interrupted the symphony. Jesse had played a crucial note completely out of tune, and Mrs. Anderson swiftly signaled for silence. The room fell quiet, and Jesse felt a rush of embarrassment wash over him. Just then, the bell rang, signaling the end of the class.

Jesse tried to slip out unnoticed, but Mrs. Anderson approached him. "Jesse," she asked calmly, "can we have a quick chat?"

"Of course," Jesse replied nervously. He followed Mrs. Anderson into her office, not knowing what to expect.

Seated at her desk, Mrs. Anderson took a sip of her tea and then asked, "Jesse, how are you feeling? You seem a bit distant lately."

Avoiding her gaze, Jesse replied, "I'm not sure, Mrs. Anderson."

"You're one of the most talented trumpeters in this class, but your recent performances have been lacking something," Mrs. Anderson noted. "And I know you practice diligently."

"I do practice every day," Jesse admitted, "but something just doesn't feel right. I don't feel connected to the music."

Mrs. Anderson nodded thoughtfully. "I see," she said. "Well, our spring recital is approaching. Have you chosen a piece to perform?"

"Not yet," Jesse confessed.

"Have you considered the Haydn piece I suggested?"

"Yeah, but I don't really like it. It's like you said—my heart isn't in it."

Jesse looked at his teacher, unsure of his next steps. He was close to backing out of the recital or even giving up on music altogether, but Mrs. Anderson spoke first.

"Alright, Jesse, take a few more days to search for a piece that resonates with you," she said sympathetically. "But since the recital is getting closer, if you don't find something soon, maybe we can give Haydn another chance, alright?"

"Okay," Jesse said half-heartedly. "Thanks, Mrs. Anderson."

"Dinner's ready!"

The scent of homemade lasagna and garlic bread filled Jesse's house. Upstairs in his room, he had been practicing for hours, but now he put down his trumpet and let out a frustrated sigh. The sheet music for the Haydn piece lay untouched on his music stand.

"Something needs to change," Jesse thought. Just then, his older sister, Lily, knocked on his door and entered.

"You've been playing beautifully," she said. "But dinner's getting cold."

Jesse managed a weak smile but still felt disheartened. Lily, noticing his frustration, put a comforting hand on his shoulder and said, "Jesse, have you ever heard of Miles Davis?"

Jesse shook his head.

"He was an incredible jazz trumpeter," Lily explained. "I think you might enjoy his music. It's different from what you've been playing, but it's so expressive and free."

Lily walked over to her record player, picked out a Miles Davis album, and played it for Jesse. The smooth jazz melodies filled the room, and Jesse realized that this was the kind of music he had been searching for. It sparked a fire within him.
"Wow, Lily," he said, giving her a grateful hug, "thank you so much. You've helped me more than you know!"

"Don't mention it," Lily replied with a smile. "Now come downstairs before dinner gets cold."

Jesse must have eaten his dinner, but his mind was elsewhere. As soon as he finished, he rushed back to his room and, instead of picking up his trumpet, sat down at his desk. He began searching for jazz sheet music, considering Miles Davis, Duke Ellington, and other jazz legends. Hearing Miles Davis had reignited his passion, and he knew what he wanted to perform.

The next day after class, Jesse eagerly approached Mrs. Anderson, a Miles Davis album in hand.

"I've found what I want to play in the concert, Mrs. A," he said, excitement in his eyes. "Have you heard of Miles Davis?"

Mrs. Anderson nodded. "Yes, I have. What is it about his music that excites you?"

Jesse paused for a moment, trying to put his feelings into words. "It feels so... free," he finally replied. "It's like he's painting with sound, and every note is a brushstroke on a canvas. I want to create music like that."

"That sounds like improvisation," Mrs. Anderson said, smiling. "It's a different world from Haydn, but it's worth exploring. We've never had jazz at our recitals before, but maybe it's time for a change."

With that, Mrs. Anderson led Jesse to the piano, and they began an impromptu jam session. Jesse felt liberated, letting the music flow through him, creating melodies on the spot. It was a feeling he had longed for, and he knew he was on the right path.

Finally, Jesse was back in tune with his music, ready to embark on a new musical journey filled with jazz, improvisation, and boundless creativity.

Comprehension Questions:

1. What role does Mrs. Anderson, Jesse's music teacher, play in his musical journey?

    a. She discourages him from pursuing jazz music.
    b. She introduces him to classical compositions.
    c. She supports and encourages his exploration of jazz.
    d. She insists he continues playing classical pieces.

2. How does Jesse's journey in the story reflect the theme of self-discovery and personal growth?

    a. By sticking to classical music, Jesse remains unchanged throughout the story.
    b. Jesse's journey showcases his resistance to change and adaptation.
    c. Through his transition to jazz and improvisation, Jesse discovers his true musical passion and creative potential.
    d. Jesse's struggles with music result in his giving up on playing altogether.

3. Read the following sentences from the text. What do you think the author was trying to tell the reader about Jesse. Choose the best answer.

    "Among the students, there was one named Jesse Reynolds, who sat in the middle of the first trumpet section. While his peers seemed to be lost in the music, soaring among the stars, Jesse felt grounded and uninspired."

    a. Jesse was having a difficult time connecting to the music.
    b. Jesse was beginning to dislike music and wants to quit.
    c. Jesse's classmates play music better than him.
    d. None of the above.

Writing prompt:

Using two details as evidence from the text, describe at least one theme of this story as it relates to the main character, Jesse.

Zooming Through Corvette History

Objective(s):
- Identify which types of figurative language and descriptive words the author used in the story, *"Zooming Through Corvette History"*.
- Construct a written response using evidence from the text that analyzes how the author's choice of figurative language adds meaning to the text.

ELA Standard(s):
- 7R4: Determine the meaning of words and phrases as they are used in a text, including figurative and connotative meanings. Analyze the impact of specific word choices on meaning, tone, and mood, including words with multiple meanings. (RL)

Essential Question:
- What makes the history of Corvettes interesting?

Target Vocabulary:
- Enthralling
- Potent
- Unconventional
- Inception
- Bona fide
- Futuristic
- Iconic
- Emissions
- Aerodynamic
- Unveiled

Introduction

Rev up your engines and fasten your seatbelts, as we embark on an exhilarating journey through time to explore the enthralling history of Corvettes. These sleek and potent sports cars have been turning heads and igniting imaginations for generations. Buckle up, and let's delve into the world of Corvettes!

Chapter 1: Birth of an Icon

Our story commences in the early 1950s when the first Corvette was unveiled by Chevrolet. It made its grand entrance at the General Motors Motorama show in New York City in 1953. The crowd was awestruck by this stunning two-seater sports car, painted in a dazzling white with a red interior.

The first-generation Corvette, often called the C1, had a fiberglass body, which was quite unconventional at the time. Under its sleek hood was a six-cylinder engine that delivered a modest 150 horsepower. While it may not have been the fastest car on the road, it was certainly one of the most stylish.

Chapter 2: Evolution of an Icon

As the years progressed, the Corvette underwent several changes and enhancements. In 1955, a V8 engine was introduced, making it a true powerhouse on the road. This was just the inception of the Corvette's transformation into a bona fide American icon.

In 1963, the Corvette Sting Ray was born, featuring a new design that was both futuristic and timeless. With its split rear window and sharp lines, it became an instant classic. Under the hood, a range of powerful V8 engines propelled the Corvette's speed to new heights.

Chapter 3: Muscle Car Madness

The 1960s and '70s were the era of muscle cars, and the Corvette was right in the thick of it. The third-generation Corvette, known as the C3, was introduced in 1968. It had bold, swooping lines and pop-up headlights that made it look like a rocket ship on wheels.
During this time, the Corvette's engines grew even more potent. The iconic small-block and big-block V8 engines gave the car astonishing speed and power. It was a time of drag races and high-speed pursuits, and the Corvette was a superstar on the streets.

Chapter 4: Adapting to Change

The 1980s and '90s brought some significant changes to the automotive world. Fuel efficiency and emissions became top priorities, which meant that sports cars had to adapt. The Corvette didn't shy away from the challenge.

In 1984, the C4 Corvette was introduced with a sleek, modern design. It featured a lightweight body and advanced technology. The introduction of the ZR-1 in 1990 showcased the Corvette's commitment to performance, with a high-revving, 375- horsepower engine, roaring like a lion on the hunt.

Chapter 5: The New Millennium

As we entered the 21st century, the Corvette continued to evolve. The C5 Corvette, introduced in 1997, was a huge step forward in terms of performance and handling. It featured an all-new, lightweight frame and a powerful LS1 V8 engine.

But the most substantial revolution came in 2005 when Chevrolet introduced the C6 Corvette. This model was packed with advanced features and offered mind-blowing performance. It had a sleek, aerodynamic design and a powerful 6.0-liter V8 engine.

Chapter 6: The Supercharged Era

In 2014, the Corvette took a giant leap forward with the introduction of the C7 Stingray. This car was not only incredibly fast but also technologically advanced. It featured a 6.2- liter V8 engine that could produce up to 650 horsepower in the Z06 model.

One of the most significant innovations was the use of lightweight materials, such as aluminum and carbon fiber, which made the Corvette even more agile and efficient. The C7 Corvette became a true supercar, capable of going head-to-head with some of the world's finest sports cars.

Chapter 7: The Future of Corvettes

As we look ahead, the Corvette's story is far from over. In 2020, Chevrolet unveiled the C8 Corvette, a groundbreaking model that shook up the sports car world. What made it so special? It was the first Corvette to feature a mid-engine layout, placing the engine behind the driver for improved balance and handling.

The C8 Corvette also introduced a new level of affordability for a mid-engine sports car, making it accessible to a broader range of enthusiasts. With a 6.2-liter V8 engine producing 490 horsepower, it was clear that the Corvette was still a force to be reckoned with.

Conclusion

The history of Corvettes is a thrilling ride through the evolution of American sports cars. From its humble beginnings in the 1950s to the high-performance machines of today, the Corvette has always represented innovation, style, and speed.

So, the next time you see a Corvette zooming down the road, remember the incredible journey it has taken to become the legendary sports car it is today. And who knows what the future holds for this iconic American symbol of power and style? Strap in and get ready for the next chapter in the history of Corvettes!

Comprehension Questions:

1. What simile was used in the text to describe the Corvette's engine sound?

    a. "Roaring like a lion on the hunt"
    b. "Sleek as a shadow in the night"
    c. "Fast as lightning on a stormy day"
    d. "Smooth as silk on a calm lake"

2. Based on the text, what might the future hold for the Corvette?
    a. It will likely disappear from the automotive market.
    b. It will continue to adapt to changing technologies and preferences.
    c. It will revert to its original design from the 1950s.
    d. It will become a luxury car brand.

3. What terms are used to describe the third-generation Corvette (C3) in the text?

    a. Sleek and technologically advanced
    b. Iconic and timeless
    c. Innovative and eco-friendly
    d. Affordable and fuel-efficient

Writing prompt:

Using examples from the text, analyze how the author's choice of figurative language adds meaning to the text.

NYS ELA Short Response Scoring Rubric

Short-response questions will ask students to make a claim, take a position, or draw a conclusion, and then support it with details. This structure forms the foundation of the Learning Standards. As such, the 2-Point Rubric focuses on both the inference and evidence a student provides. This structure allows students to have wide latitude in responding to each prompt so long as their response is supported by the text. Additionally, the expectation for all short responses will be complete, coherent sentences. By weaving these elements together, the questions, responses, and scores remain firmly focused on student reading ability.

2-Point Rubric—Short Response

Points	Response features
2	The features of a 2-point response are: • Valid inferences and/or claims from the text where required by the prompt • Evidence of analysis of the text where required by the prompt • Relevant facts, definitions, concrete details, and/or other information from the text to develop response according to the requirements of the prompt • Sufficient number of facts, definitions, concrete details, and/or other information from the text as required by the prompt • Complete sentences where errors do not impact readability
1	The features of a 1-point response are: • A mostly literal recounting of events or details from the text as required by the prompt • Some relevant facts, definitions, concrete details, and/or other information from the text to develop response according to the requirements of the prompt • Incomplete sentences or bullets
0	The features of a 0-point response are: • A response that does not address any of the requirements of the prompt or is totally inaccurate • A response that is not written in English • A response that is unintelligible or indecipherable

Made in the USA
Middletown, DE
30 March 2024